BEFORE

THE

SHOT

SHAREE A. SMITH

Forward by:
Pastor Pamela Rozier

© 2020 by Sharee A. Smith

Scripture quotations are taken from the *Holy Bible*, New Living Translation, copyright ©1996, 2004, 2007 by Tyndale House Foundation; the *Holy Bible,* King James Version. New York: American Bible Society: 1999 Holy Bible, King James Version, copyright © 1999 by New York: Bible Society; and the *Holy Bible,* Amplified Version, *Copyright © 2015.*

Printed in the United States of America

THIS BOOK IS NOT INTENDED TO BE A HISTORY TEXT. While every effort has been made to check the accuracy of dates, locations, and historical information, no claims are made as to the accuracy of such information.

For book orders, author appearance inquires and interviews, contact the author:

ISBN-13: 978-1-7365810-1-8

Contact the Author

www.Shareesmith.com

FaceBook: Sharee A. Smith
IG: @shareestscsl

Dudley Publishing
HOUSE

www.dudleypublishinghouse.net
Submissions@dudleypublishinghouse.net

Dedication

This book is dedicated to marriages that have lost hope and who are looking to heal their hopeless heart.

Acknowledgments

First and foremost I want to thank my husband, Jerron Smith for his willingness to be transparent and open with sharing his very personal experiences for this book, as well as our martial experiences. It was not easy as we opened up to one another in order to allow healing and rebuilding to come forth in our marriage. To God be all the glory for what was birthed in our marriage through this book.

I also would like to personally thank Mr. Keith and Mrs. Pamela Rozier for their tireless efforts in helping my husband and me work through some tough situations in our marriage. I also want to send a very special shout out to Mrs. Angel Paloade for her expert advice that she provided to my husband and me in our individual therapy sessions and marriage counseling. Your words of life put meaning back into our marriage. A special thank you to Mrs. Jasmine Dudley for the push and encouragement during this book writing process. The wisdom you poured into me helped to birth Before the Shot.

Foreword

By: Pastor Pamela Rozier

Before I say anything, I would like to thank Jerron and Sharee Smith for trusting the Holy Spirit to lead my husband and myself, as we guided them through the troubled waters of marriage. They chose to open up their hearts to the Word of GOD and allowed the Truth to penetrate through the lies that the devil used in attempts to destroy their union. Marriage is definitely work and in reading this book you will see the effort they put forth to dismantle the devices Satan used to infiltrate their marriage. The Bible tells us in Hebrews 13:4 that marriage is honorable in all and the bed undefiled. If we know that GOD honors marriage, we should honor GOD in our marriage. While this book talks about the shots that the devil fired at their marriage, GOD used His invisible Shield of FAITH and the Breastplate of Righteousness to block the attack! They were able to put on the Amour of GOD mentioned in Ephesians 6:10-18 to withstand Satan's shots. Jerron and Sharee now understand the difference between the blank shots and real ammunition that was shot from the devil's gun.

The Bible also says that we should give no place to the devil – Ephesians 4:27, meaning, we cannot allow ourselves to be used by Satan. James 4:7 tells us to submit ourselves therefore to GOD. Resist the devil, and he will flee from you. Before the Shot will show married couples and anyone aspiring to be married, how to submit to the Will of GOD to combat every lie from devil and every negative word that he has spoken over their marriage or relationship. Sharee and Jerron's experiences has helped them to overcome some tough situations that were designed to destroy their union. Their desire to trust God through the process was so inspirational that it inspired Sharee to write this masterpiece to teach other couples how to endure the rough seasons of marriage. You will learn what it means to keep each other lifted up in prayer and how to stand on the Word of God for your marriage. Mark 10:9 says, therefore what GOD has join together, let no man separate.

I am so Godly proud of the growth that I have witnessed in Jerron and Sharee, and their endeavors to trust GOD, no matter what! I pray that this book will save marriages across the World and help them to understand that their fight is not against each other. Husband, wives, and those who aspire to be married must come together to understand its spiritual warfare against Satan and his kingdom and his attack on marriages. The Bible states in 2 Corinthians 10:4-6 that, for the weapons of our warfare are not carnal, but mighty through God to the pulling down of strong holds. Casting down imaginations, and every high thing that exalt itself against the knowledge of God, and bringing into captivity every thought to the obedience of Christ; and having in a readiness to revenge all disobedience, when your obedience is fulfilled. This scripture is a clear indication that married couples must see the devil for who he is, work together with their spouse to defeat him and kick him out of their union! As I close, my prayer is that you and your spouse stand on the Word of God and the scripture found in Ecclesiastes 4:12 – And if one prevail against him, two shall withstand him; and a threefold cord is not quickly broken. The devil won't win when you have God as the third cord!

Table of Contents

Introduction………………………………..13

1st Bullet – The Past……………………...21

- Things that hindered us from becoming one in the flesh.

2nd bullet – Undealt with Rejection……….35

- The rejection from our past that carried over nto our marriage.

3rd bullet – Trust Issues…………………..47

- The distrust that caused us to question the reliability of our union.

Intermission…………………………….56

Call to Action Activities and Exercises…58

4th Bullet - Rebuilding God's Way………...71

- Using the word of God to lead to the road of recovery

5th bullet - Communication is Key………..81

- Relearning the art of communication

6th Bullet - Two is Better than One……….89

- Joining forces to fight the problem, not one another.

<u>Introduction</u>

What do you think of when you hear the word "shot?" Do you think about the point guard who just dropped a three-point shot from half-court at the buzzer to win the game of his or her career? Do you think about the round of shots you paid for at the bar last night while celebrating your best friend's birthday? What about your big shot co-worker that just got a promotion for a job well done? You may have even thought about the shot your child received from the doctor. Or the gunshots you heard in the alleyway while sitting on the restaurant rooftop in the city. Well, when I think of the word "shot", I think about the shot the devil took at the heart of my marriage. He had his gun locked and loaded, firing off several rounds of bullets that were intended to kill the very core of a union that God joined in holy matrimony. Although God declared in His word in *Mark 10:9 that what He joined together, let no man separate* or come in between, that didn't stop the devil from trying his best to take us both out emotionally, mentally, physically, and spiritually. This declaration also meant that you are not to allow no woman, child, thing, or even Satan to get during your marriage and tear it up.

From the time my husband and I started dating, the issues arose. Some of you may ask the question "why did we move forward with getting married?" God's assurance of knowing our union was ordained by Him helped us to decide to push through the obstacles. When your love for one another is greater than any bullet that's being shot from the devil's gun, you can press past your reality or current circumstance. When you can visualize the bigger picture and purpose for your marriage, you won't let "life hitting" stop you from achieving happiness and a successful marriage. This book came into fruition one day as I sat back in thought about how I survived my abusive first marriage to now striving to obtain a healthy second marriage that is built on the foundation and principles of Christ. We all envision a loving fulfilled healthy marriage with God as the centerpiece. However, Life comes into play and shatters that beautiful image that was once pictured. You are left with the broken pieces of your heart, not knowing how or if they will be mended. With God at the forefront of your marriage, it is possible to come together in the way that it is meant to be.

I started writing this book with the realization that I'm not the only one going through some of the things I was experiencing within my marriage. Some people may be going through similar situations but can't seem to put into words their thoughts. With that being said, what a perfect reason to share with other couples my personal defeats and triumphs. Marriage is not easy and like the cliché "there is no manual on how to raise a child", well there is no manual on the perfect marriage. Many people have written about what they think a good marriage is and how to obtain one. But the truth is, how can an imperfect person write about having a perfect marriage? Perfection doesn't exist in humans who are flawed by nature. The bible says that *we are shaped in iniquity and in sin did our mother conceived us – Psalm 51:5.* God's grace is enough for our life, and it is in our weakness that our strength is made perfect. So, if we lean on Him during those rough patches in our marriages, He will uphold us with His right hand. *He will also lift up a standard when the enemy come in like a flood! (Isaiah 59:19)*

My husband and I were dealing with some of the same root issues that we never noticed until our happiness came to a screeching halt. Thinking about my marriage, I want to be transparent in exposing the different areas that the devil used in attempts to destroy us. We both carried baggage from our past that hindered us from becoming one flesh as God intended. The seed of rejection from our insecurities spilled over into our union, causing us to become emotionally withdrawn, distant, and disengaged. The distrust that we had towards one another made us not fully trust each other's intentions. There were always questions in the back of our minds, wondering if we were truly vested in the marriage. The lack of communication left angry conversations playing over and over in our minds, thinking about what we should have said during the heat of the argument.

We had to relearn the art of communicating with a response from what was being said, instead of reacting first to what we heard. Our perceptions and views were shaped by all the negative experiences we both endured before we met. We had to go through the process of "unlearning bad behaviors" that caused division in our home. It was a funny thing how the light bulb came on at the same time for both of us. We finally realized that two is better than one, which meant we had to learn to fight the problems together instead of fighting one another.

While you are reading Before the Shot, I want you and your significant other to discover how you relate to some of my personal marital experiences. This will require you to dig deep into those dark places of your heart that you don't frequently visit. Your honesty is the most powerful tool that will bring healing to your marriage as you explore the root of your pain, whether it came from your childhood or a recent relationship breakup. Being set free means that you must become totally vulnerable and naked to yourself first and then to your spouse. Those walls that you have built up and around your heart must come down so that your spouse will be able to penetrate the layers without resistance and hesitation. He or she must know that they are in a safe space to do so without fear of retaliation. No one said that this would be an easy task, but with commitment and perseverance, it can and will be achieved! The fight to press on must come from within for both parties involved. There must be a willingness to have each other's back no matter how ugly "the process" may get. Remember the vows you took before God, family, and friends said, "for better, for worse, for richer, for poorer, in sickness and health, until death do us part." *Ecclesiastes 5:5 says better is it that thou should not vow than that thou should vow and not pay.*

When we honor God in our marriage as the first strand of the three-strand cord that holds our marriage together, we cannot fail. His Word is the glue that will keep the bond solid and unbreakable. Weapons may form, but they shall not prosper because of the hope in Christ Jesus that your union is built on. Having that "Now Faith" that is mentioned in *Hebrews 11:1* will be the catalyst to carry your ship through the storms of life. As you and your spouse stand on the promises of God, you will come to understand if God be for you, He is more than the world who is against you – Romans 8:31. I pray that this book brings healing, restoration, and peace to your marriage. May it open doors for you to be able to share your testimony to help other couples. Always keep in mind that nothing we go through is for us but is always for someone else and for God to get the glory out of our lives. He can take two imperfect people and make them perfect for one another! No marriage is perfect but what looks impossible to man is possible with God as your anchor.

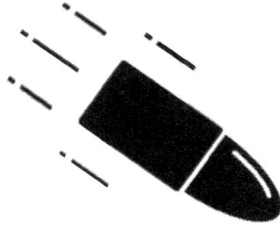

Bullet 1

The Past

Things That Hindered Us from Becoming One in the Flesh

Before you dive into what hindered my marriage, I thought it necessary to explain to you the anatomy of a bullet and the damage it causes. A bullet is defined by Merriam-Webster Dictionary as a round or elongated missile (as of lead) to be fired from a firearm broadly. It has four components- the casing, the primer, the powder, and the projectile (which we can now call the bullet). The casing is the container that holds the other three components together when the trigger is fired. The primer sits at the rim of the casing and serves as the place that your gun's firing pin will hit once the trigger is pulled. The powder has only one job and that is to get burnt. The burning takes place with the tight, concealed spacing of the cartridge, which causes rapid expansion and enormous pressure. As the primer and powder ignite, an explosive force of gas travels through the chamber of a gun, pushing the bullet in one direction, its projected target. When a person is shot and the bullet enters their body, it not only pierces through their skin tissue, it also shatters bones and tears through the muscle. Now with this in mind, imagine the devil holding his gun and his primary target is the heart of your marriage. He is a skilled marksman who shoots rounds and rounds of bullets into every hole and weakness he can penetrate during spiritual warfare, which is usually your point of vulnerability. The marriages that are not equipped with their spiritual armor become casualties of war. But for those unions who are equipped, can withstand the fight.

Our past is one of the bullets that the devil used against us in his studious effort to destroy our unification and separate us from the love of God. The past only symbolizes who we used to be compared to who we are now. Our past can only shape us, not define us. One might ask how did we move forward holding on to what was behind us? The obvious answer to that question is we couldn't. The devil took the irrelevant baggage of our past to hinder our forward progression in God. These emotional scars and traumas permanently damaged our natural minds. But when we accepted Christ as our Lord and Savior and began to walk in the things of Him, we were healed in the spiritual realm. Although we carried the residue of brokenness in the natural realm of life, His healing was made manifest through our growth and maturity in the things of the spirit. My husband and I sought out practical and spiritual guidance to gain an understanding of how and why our past constantly showed up in our marriage. The devil was very strategic in his approach to take us down. As you continue reading, you will see the different areas he attacked.

The "Emotional Baggage" Shell Casing

The breakdown started in the third year of us being joined in holy matrimony. My mother's decision to move to town brought about many mismatched emotions. Whilst I was happy that she was here with me and my children, there were unresolved emotions that were lingering from a trauma I experienced in my childhood which I'd never discussed with her. Shortly after her arrival, God began to deal with me regarding this trauma. I was forced to face my inner demons that I hide from everyone, including her. Being in my mother's presence reminded me of the person who violated me. It was one of her former boyfriends who lived with us when I was five years old. For the life of me, I could not bring myself to tell my mother what happened to me, so I purposely avoided getting close to her at that moment. My innocence was stolen from me by the bullet of molestation and blaming her was easier than dealing with the anger and hurt I was internally suffering from. This drove a wedge into our already fragile relationship. My constant denial and dismissal of the molestation and the avoidance of my truth caused me to have an emotional breakdown. It was then that I realized I needed to seek out help to deal with the weight I had been carrying since I was a little child.

My husband, on the other hand, had his own demons he was fighting. There were several traumas from his past that hindered him but I'm going to discuss the one that impacted his life the most. My husband realized that he needed help with his emotional baggage when the bad behaviors he attempted to suppress in every relationship he had before me, started to creep up in our marriage. He witnessed his father's cycle of drug abuse over the years, not fully understanding how it would negatively affect him academically, behaviorally, emotionally, and socially. The chaos going on in his mind opened the door to his insecurities, which made him seek approval from others. He carried a passive-aggressive communication style that made him resentful for not having the courage to be direct and honest with people. The pandemonium also made it hard for him to say "no" to people which caused him to live their life instead of his own.

Lastly, he wore a mask of denial which made it impossible for him to form intimate, fulfilling relationships. This cycle of defeat sent him into a tailspin that truly affected his growth as a man. Feeling like you have no one to turn to in your desperation will lead you down a path of sin, full of arrogance and pride. My husband was crying out for help just as I was. As the silent tears fell with great disparity, we both failed to see one another's brokenness. We were two incomplete vessels that needed to learn how to harness our negative emotions and be made whole.

Learning to Harness Negative Emotions

If you and your spouse are going to move forward from your past, you must learn to harness those negative emotions that cause bad behaviors. We often allow our emotions to get the best of us in any given situation. Not that you're wrong for having negative emotions, it's how you deal with them. When you or your spouse are operating out of emotion, you are using tools of the devil, causing issues to go unresolved. A good example that portrays both negative and positive emotion in the bible is found in *Matthew 26:36-46* when Jesus was in the garden praying with His disciples before Judas betrayed Him. Jesus expressed to them that "His soul is exceedingly sorrowful". The emotion was not expressed in a dispassionate way. The disciples clearly understood that He was displeased with them for their failure to stay woke and pray with Him. As Jesus continued praying to His Father in Heaven, He was able to accept God's will for His life. This acceptance shifted His emotional disposition from negative to positive.

When we are in platonic relationships with others, whether it's a marriage or a friendship, we must learn to mirror Jesus. We must learn to acknowledge our emotions, work through the process of each emotion, and then release those negative feelings without internalizing them. Internalizing simply means that you do not hold on to negative thoughts and allow them to cause you to overthink the situation or the process to get through it. If you allow yourself to fall into internalizing your negative emotions, unsatisfactory behaviors such as anxiety, depression, loneliness, sadness, and withdrawal will follow. So, it's very important that you learn to recognize the symptoms of negative emotions and use the Word of God to combat them. Please read and apply the scriptures below to your marriage if you or your spouse deal with any of the negative behaviors listed above:

Anxiety

- *Matthew 11:28 Come to me, all you who labor and are heavy laden, and I will give you rest.*
- *Philippians 4:6-7 Be anxious for nothing, but in everything, by prayer and supplication, with thanksgiving, let your requests be made known to God; and the peace of God, which surpasses all understanding, will guard your hearts and minds through Christ Jesus.*
- *1 Peter 5:7 cast all your care upon Him, for He cares for you.*

Depression

- *Romans 8:38-39 For I am persuaded that neither death nor life, nor angels, nor principalities, nor powers, nor things present nor things to come, nor height nor depth, nor any other created thing, shall be able to separate us from the love of God which is in Christ Jesus our Lord.*
- *II Corinthians 1:3-4 blessed be the God and Father of our Lord Jesus Christ, the Father of mercies and God of all comfort, who comforts us in all our tribulation that we may be able to comfort those who are in any trouble, with the comfort with which we ourselves are comforted by God.*

Loneliness

- *Psalm 17:15 as for me, I will see your face in righteousness; I shall be satisfied when I awake in your likeness.*
- *Colossians 3:1-4 if then you were raised with Christ, seek those things which are above, where Christ is, sitting at the right hand of God. Set your mind on things above, not on things on the earth. For you died, and your life is hidden with Christ in God. When Christ who is our life appears when you also will appear with Him in glory.*

Sadness

- *Psalm 3:3 but you, O Lord, are a shield about me, my glory, and the lifter of my head.*
- *Psalm 30:5 for his anger is but for a moment, and his favor is for a lifetime. Weeping may endure or the night, but joy comes with the morning.*

Withdrawal

- *Psalm 34:1-19 the righteous cry, and the LORD hears and delivers them out of all their troubles. The LORD is nigh unto them that are of a broken heart, and saves such as be of a contrite spirit. Many are the afflictions of the righteous: but the LORD delivers him out of them all.*
- *Isiah 54:17 No weapon that is formed against thee shall prosper, and every tongue that shall rise against thee in judgment thou shalt condemn. This is the heritage of the servants of the LORD, and their righteousness is of me, saith the LORD.*

The "Blame" Shell Casing

Blame is a shell casing that hindered my husband and me from being able to love one another the way God loved us. We both fell victim to the blame game in an attempt to justify why we were fighting with one another. This very action meant that we were stuck in our past and were not willing to let go of the reigns. He thought his feelings were more important than mine and I surely thought my feelings were greater than his. Most of our arguments ended with neither of us accepting blame for how they began. The lack of accepting the blame caused fear to arise, a fear that prevented us from taking risks within our marriage, and a fear of taking responsibility. Blame also caused feelings of resentment towards one another, increased emotional stress, and a decreased desire to communicate effectively. Yelling and screaming became the "norm" for us.

We were on separate pages when it came to the issues. There were times where my husband wanted to work towards a solution to the problem while I continued finger-pointing and vice versa. Bad behaviors like these rendered us both powerless in finding a resolve and ultimately destroyed our passion and intimacy for each other. I was on the frontline, standing my ground on my viewpoints and so was he. Be-low-the-belt shots were fired as if the opponent was a stranger. Spiritually speaking, the real enemy was the devil, but we failed to see this because we were blinded by pride. Our bedroom served its purpose as a war zone when it should have been a place of peace and intimacy!

Putting the Blame Game to Shame

If you are not careful, continued blame usage will cause you to feel a false sense of protection while your spouse is left unprotected and exposed. The worst thing a person that doesn't want to change can do is not take responsibility for anything, not even their own faults. You are left alone, center stage for all to see. There are three key essentials you can use to "silence" the blame:

- Confess your sins to God – Confession is not designed to bring shame and guilt. Those are tools of the devil. Confession shines the light on sin that is present in our life. Once it is exposed, God can perform the work to clean you up. (*I John 1:9 But if we confess our sins to him, he is faithful and just to forgive us our sins and to cleanse us from all wickedness.*)

- Refrain from blaming your spouse – it is a sign of disrespect and rejection, also tools of the devil, which hinders freedom and forgiveness to take place within the marriage. (*Matthew 7:3-5 And why worry about a speck in your friend's eye when you have a log in your own? How can you think of saying to your friend, 'Let me help you get rid of that speck in your eye,' when you can't see past the log in your own eye? Hypocrite! First, get rid of the log in your own eye; then you will see well enough to deal with the speck in your friend's eye.*)

- Do not play the blame game, by any means necessary – this will only perpetuate your emotions and cause arguments to escalate, sometimes to the point of no return. So, choose your words wisely, for a gentle answer turns away wrath while a hard answer stirs up anger and strife. (*Romans 16:17 And now I make one more appeal, my dear brothers and sisters. Watch out for people who cause divisions and upset people's faith by teaching things contrary to what you have been taught. Stay away from them.)*

Take Away

I want to leave you with this final thought on dealing with the emotional baggage of your past and blame. It is a true statement to say that every negative and traumatic encounter you went through, stained your memory, which in turn, dulled your perception on how you view the positive experiences in your life. In order to bring about a change in your marriage, you must be willing to release the negative emotional truth that you created from the experience. These occurrences do not govern your future, nor do they have the final say in your life! *Jeremiah 29:11 clearly states that God's thoughts He thinks towards you, are thoughts of peace and not evil, to give you a future and a hope.* Paul, one of Jesus' greatest disciples, stated in *Philippians 3:12-14 that you should forget those things which are behind you (the past) and press toward the goal for the prize of the upward call of God in Christ Jesus. Finally, we must remember, Satan is an accuser of the brethren (Revelation 12:10).* If you and your spouse allow the spirit of pride to operate in your life, you will be a continual accuser of your brother/sister like Satan. The bible says in *Proverbs 16:18 that pride goes before destruction and a haughty spirit before a fall.* Humility goes a long way with God and taking the low road will unlock doors within your marriage that the devil will never be able to close!

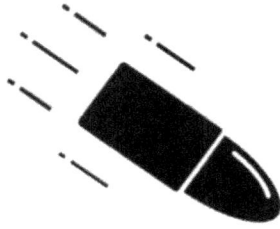

Bullet 2

Undealt with Rejection

The Rejection From Our Past That Carried Over
Into Our Marriage

Rejection is something that we all have experienced in some way, shape, or form, whether it was parental or sibling rejection, social rejection, or relationship rejection. It shows up in your life if you have ever experienced any type of abuse, anxiety, depression, stress, or trauma. When the devil fires his gun, the bullet of rejection penetrates your soul and shatters your self-confidence, self-esteem, self-value, and self-worth. You are left feeling empty, always wondering if you are enough. Rejection eats away at the very core of who you are. Compromising, easily making negative assumptions, showing an unwillingness to give and receive love, and suspicious of letting others in, are all attributes of rejection that are not as noticeable by the people around you. The biggest and most outwardly attribute of them all is seen in a person who is a people pleaser. If you or your spouse identify with one or more of these bad behaviors, you more than likely deal with rejection. The bullet of rejection is the number one strategy that he uses to destroy your marriage. Here is something to think about - if the devil can keep you bound up with rejection, how will you and your spouse ever become one?

My battle with rejection started in my childhood and continued well into my adulthood. This bullet penetrated my soul as a child, carrying with it, my need to be accepted by my family. I was a person who thought I was unlovable. It also made me think that I wasn't enough. So, I spent my teenage years and a lot of my adult years searching and yearning for acceptance by those around me. Some of the people in my life during this time only tolerated me but never really wanted to deal with me and accept me for who I was. They saw the seed of rejection operating in me but instead of praying with me and for me, they too rejected me like so many others had done from my past. I was flawed and broken, longing to be validated by others.

Many nights were spent crying and questioning God about why people rejected me. This bullet stayed lodged into my soul until God delivered me. I will never forget the day God dislodged it from my soul. I was sitting in the bathtub listening to Overcome by Tye Tribbett. As the lyrics ministered to my spirit, I heard the Lord speak to me so audibly through the song, "all authority, every victory is yours". Tears began to flow down my cheeks as God continued speaking to me. He told me that because of my praise He was setting me free from rejection and that I no longer needed to seek validation from others. By this time, I'd gotten up out of the tub and begin praising God right there in my bathroom! I was finally free from something that had me weighted down for most of my life.

My husband's rejection stemmed from being rejected as a child by his father. He did not receive the same attention as his younger brothers. The praise that his siblings received, passed him by. I remember my husband sharing a story with me of how his dad never came out to support him at any of his football and basketball games. Can you imagine looking up in the stands after you scored a touchdown and seeing no one there to cheer you on? Imagine the feeling of hearing your dad down-play your talent and love for sports. How would that make you feel? My husband felt alone and sometimes feelings of abandonment came over him, leaving an empty space in his heart. The lack of support caused him to quit something that he loved so much. Not getting the well-deserved recognition from his dad caused him to also seek validation from others. He also resorted to self-gratification, meaning he aimed to gratify whatever impulse he had at that moment. He, like myself, felt as if he wasn't good enough. As he grew up and became a man, he realized that the rejection he experienced caused him not to really put forth an effort with anything, which resulted in him doing just enough to get by. He lost his zeal and passion for the simple things in life.

The bullet of rejection stunted my husband's maturity and growth as a man. It seemed as if his dad didn't really care about him. There was no push to excel or reach for the next level in life. Maybe his father didn't know how to be that hands-on dad that he needed, especially with my husband being the eldest son. His parents put a lot of unwanted responsibility on him to look after his younger siblings. Their father and son relationship was built on the shaky grounds of no fatherly guidance in certain areas of his life and lack of support. Now that you have the back story of how rejection affected us both individually, let's move into how it negatively impacted our marriage.

The "Masking" Shell Casing

Let me set the scene for you. Here we are standing at the altar, after two years of dating, saying our "I do's" before God and our family and friends. He's dressed in his navy-blue suit with a cream-colored button-down dress shirt with gold cufflinks and some brown Stacey Adams. The colors in his bowtie represented the color scheme of our wedding. I was dressed in a creamed-colored contemporary wedding dress where the length hung just below my knees. My ears and wrist were adorned with rose-gold accessories. The rose-gold stiletto heels I had on, completed the look I wanted. I didn't wear a traditional veil; I wore a fascinator that was made with mesh netting and pearls the same color as my dress. We looked absolutely stunning on our special day. But the one thing that no one saw was the invisible masks that we both were wearing.

The pain we both experienced from the bullet of rejection was hidden behind our masks. I know you are probably thinking at this point did we went through pre-marital counseling. We did! The counseling only dealt with the major components of marriage such as finances, belief system, children, blended family, and the biblical expectations of a husband and wife. It did not deal with those hidden intricacies that you don't want anyone to find out about. So, we pretended and masqueraded around in our marriage as you do at a masquerade ball for the first two years.

One key thing we failed to realize was that the devil was laying low and waiting for the perfect opportunity to take his shot. Work absorbed my husband's days and his nights were filled with Facebook browsing until he fell asleep, which left no time for intimacy. This is something that all couples need to sustain a healthy marriage. No, sex is not everything, but it is important! Most nights I would lie in bed wondering if he really wanted me. It appeared he didn't. Not receiving attention from my husband caused feelings of aloneness. I could not bring myself to talk about the rejection to anyone. The shame silenced my speech.

We were newlyweds only three years in and already having issues because of the un-dealt with rejection we both were carrying. Now, the rejection I sent his way was a little different. The very first time we did couples therapy, we were introduced to "The 5 Love Languages". It is an interactive website that help you to discover the top three out of five love languages your partner needed to feel loved. My love languages are Gifts, Quality Time, and Acts of Service. His love languages are Physical Touch, Quality Time, and Words of Affirmation. Knowing that he required my physical touch, I didn't always oblige. A physical touch meant anything from a daily hug and kiss to a pat on the back. I failed miserably with this task. Our dating stage started out with these individual love languages, but after we crossed the marriage threshold, they dimin-ished over time. And we can thank the bullet of rejection and the masking shell casing for this! The lack of my physical touch made him feel rejected and he too, lay in bed at night wondering if I wanted him. Couples therapy revealed our horrible truth, forcing the masks to be removed for a season. Things would be going good until the devil decided to shoot another round of rejection our way from the pains of our pasts. Once again, the devil's tools were at work, and as a result of this, we both put on our invisible masks as if we were okay.

Removing the Masks

You might think that this task is not possible. But for healing to come forth, it is a requirement by God. Removing your mask means that you are willing to become vulnerable before your spouse and you are no longer worried about how you will be viewed by them. This symbolic gesture forces you into a life of freedom. The human side of us loves to hold on to what's familiar to us as if it were a security blanket. When we are striving to grow and evolve, we must travel into unknown territories. This is where you can grab a hold of God's unchanging hand and allow Him to lead and guide you through this unmarked terrain. God reassures us of His leading in *Psalm 119:105 where He says His word is a lamp unto our feet and a light to our path.* Removing your masks requires you to have the patience of Job and humility of Jesus. No pride can be found in you when taking off your mask. And this is what the bible speaks about if you refuse to humble yourself – *Pride goes before destruction and a haughty spirit before a fall (Proverbs 16:18).* If you want to give your marriage any hope of healing, you must throw your mask shell casings away.

Five Things That Happen When You Remove the Mask and Deal with Rejection

1. **You no longer avoid new opportunities** – the fear that came with the spirit of rejection is no longer present in your life.
2. **People pleasing comes to an end** – you now have the courage to say "no" without feeling guilty.
3. **You close the curtain to disingenuous public performances** – you no longer live in fear of your spouse discovering the "real you."
4. **You learn to speak up** – you finally learned the art of passivity by accepting

what happens without active response and resistance.

5. **Passive-aggressive behavior is no longer a part of you** – you stop using the devil's tool of manipulation to get what you want with bribing and trickery.

Take Away

I have concluded that masking and rejection are two things that will destroy your marriage if you continue avoiding their existence in your life. Neither is easy to overcome, but the key to overcoming is recognizing and accepting that you suffer from both, confessing the recognition, trusting that God will walk you through your deliverance. There were several passages of scripture that assisted me and my husband with overcoming masking and rejection. But the one that we stood on throughout the process was Psalm 23. And in standing on God's word, the bullet of rejection was dislodged from the soul of our marriage, causing our masks to be removed.

A Psalm of David

The Lord is my shepherd; I shall not want. He makes me to lie down in green pastures; He leads me beside the still waters. He restores my soul; He leads me in the paths of righteousness For His name's sake. Yea, though I walk through the valley of the shadow of death, I will fear no evil; For You are with me; Your rod and Your staff, they comfort me You prepare a table before me in the presence of my enemies; You anoint my head with oil; My cup runs over. Surely goodness and mercy shall follow me all the days of my life, and I will dwell in the house of the Lord Forever.

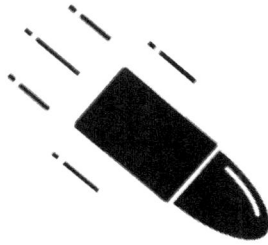

Bullet 3

Trust Issues

The Distrust that Caused Us to Question the Reliability of Our Union

Whew......trust and distrust, two topics that can be difficult to discuss in any marriage. To provide you with a better understanding of this chapter, let's breakdown the meaning of each word. According to the Oxford Languages Dictionary, distrust is defined as the feeling that someone or something cannot be relied upon; doubt the honesty or reliability of; regard with suspicion. Trust is defined by this same dictionary as having a firm belief in the reliability, truth, ability, or strength of someone or something. When I think about the two definitions, my interpretation is this: one meaning shows that whatever you are or were building wasn't built on a solid foundation and the other meaning shows that you are or were building on a solid foundation. Now we know that anything that does not have a sure foundation is prone to be shot down by the devil. How do you think the devil knows when you are building on rocky ground? Think for a minute....... the answer to this question is- you are using his tools, that's how he knows. So once again, he travels back to your past to reload his gun.

The unresolved issues from our past spilled over into our marriage, causing the spirit of distrust to infiltrate the foundation of the God-ordained union. The devil understood that when I was violated as a child, I would grow up not being able to trust people. He understood that the rejection my husband experienced as a child would make him question the reliability of any platonic relationship he entered. These being the main reasons why it was easy for the devil to shoot the bullet of distrust into the soul of your marriage. The shell casings of doubt, distortion, and division were the evidence that trust issues existed. And because the warning and detour signs were ignored, the bullets fired from the devil's gun pierced with such a force that almost wiped out our fragile union. And most times when he aimed, he seldom missed his target. Let's Segway into how the devil used the triple threat – doubt, distortion, and division as an assassination attempt on my marriage.

The "Doubt" Shell Casing

Remember in Bullet 1 I talked about the start of the breakdown of our marriage. Well, let me tell you what happened when we stopped trusting God. Our traumatic experiences from the past added to our trust issues. The trauma we experienced in our first marriages left a negative imprint in our minds. Failed romantic relationships broke each of our hearts into a million pieces. The rejection from family members caused an unbearable hurt in our souls. Being sexually violated negatively impacted my childhood innocence. Him being lied to by a girl who pinned a baby on him that wasn't his, caused my husband to have a trust issue with women. Neither of us trusted anyone! The mind of a person who does not trust believes that it won't get done unless they do it. They also believe that they must rely on themselves to make things happen. And this is exactly how we thought. Different attributes of doubt were hidden in many areas of our life: past experiences – certain characteristics portrayed by each of us triggered a blocked memory; stress and anticipation – this double whammy caused many misunderstandings between my husband and me; fear – set an unrealistic expectation on us in thinking that we would make sure everything goes right; insecurities – we constantly blamed my one another for everything and was always in a battle to control the narrative. The result made us doubt one another and made us feel as if we couldn't rely on one another. Does any of this sound familiar to you?

The "Distortion" Shell Casing

Trauma caused us to view our marriage through distorted lenses. Coming from a past filled with dysfunction, distorted my reality as well as my husband's reality. Relational pain distorted our views of one another. The person we wanted from each other conflicted with the person that was being showcased. We both suffered from faulty mental filters that provoked self-doubt and had us overreacting to our partner's intent. My constant overreacting and assuming caused my husband to become withdrawn and quiet. My distorted thinking made me think he was neglecting me which triggered my low self-esteem. It wasn't that he was neglecting me, he could have had a bad day at work and didn't feel like engaging with me as I perpetuated the argument. Now his distorted way of thinking made him view me the same way he viewed the bad behaviors of women from his past. Although I did not behave as they did, some of my negative characteristics triggered his bad memories of these women. When weariness set in from battling one another through a distorted lens, we pushed away from each other instead of bonding.

The "Division" Shell Casing

Matthew 12:25 says that a house divided against itself cannot stand. The division in our marriage didn't happen overnight, it happened over a period of time that was fueled by busyness, small disagreements, uncompromising stubbornness, misplaced priorities, unmet expectations, and the lack of communication.

Pride and selfish intentions are the root cause of division and often dictated how my husband and I engaged with each other. Our continued inwardly focus and refusal to reconcile meant that we failed to recognize that we were responding to one another in a spirit of self-preservation. If we did not change this behavior, this would be the dissolution of our marriage. The marital division is likened to the splitting of a cell nucleus; it causes an unstoppable chain reaction. My husband and I did not understand the consequences of division. We did not realize that we were better together.

The marital strife in our marriage quickly became the start of the "D" word – DIVORCE. I knew in my heart of hearts that I didn't want a divorce, but I was exhausted from the warfare. He is the one who brought up the "D" word every time we argued which made me assume that he really wanted out. Our pride, along with stubbornness, anger, bitterness, hurt, and frustration prevented us from communicating effectively. If we were ever going to sever the tie of division, we had to figure out a way to talk to one another. Now that you have insight into how the triple threat can ruin a marriage, I want to share with you the stages of distrust and how to combat them. Knowing these stages will help you recognize when distrust is present within yourself and within your union. One thing I love about God is that He will not leave us ignorant of Satan's devices. He will always send a warning before anything happens. Obey your premonition!

Five Stages of Distrust

1. **Doubt**
   - **Confidence** kills doubt. *Proverbs 3:26 For the LORD shall be thy* **confidence** *and shall keep thy foot from being taken*

2. **Suspicion**
   - **Assurance** kills suspicion. *Hebrews 10:22 Let us draw near with a sincere heart in full* **assurance** *of faith, having our hearts sprinkled clean from an evil conscience and our bodies washed with pure water.*

3. **Anxiety**
   - **Peace** kills anxiety. *Philippians 4:7 And the* **peace** *of God, which surpasses all understanding, will guard*

your hearts and minds through Christ Jesus.

4. **Fear**

- **Tranquility in knowing** God is always with us kills fear. *Isaiah 43:2 When thou pass through the waters,* **I will be with thee;** *and through the rivers, and they shall not overflow thee: when thou walk through the fire, thou shalt not be burned; neither shall the flame kindle upon thee.*

5. **Self-Preservation**

- **Self-Denial** kills self-preservation. *Matthew 16:24 Then Jesus said to His disciples, "If anyone wishes to come after Me, he must deny himself, and take up his cross and follow Me.*

Take-Away

Here is where we missed it. God told us in His word that we should *trust in Him with all your heart and lean not on your own understanding; in all your ways acknowledge Him, And He shall direct your paths – Proverbs 3:5-6.* If you haven't noticed by now that your past is the culprit that opens the door for the devil to take shots at your marriage. Not getting delivered from your past creates vulnerability within your union. The devil knows he can go to war on a marriage that has weaknesses. The only way to dispel distrust and prevent the bullet from shattering your marriage is to proactively build your foundation on TRUST. It must be nurtured and continuously developed throughout your marriage and in your individual lives. Trust is the weapon that will jam the devil's gun. So, fire TRUST back at him!

Intermission

The devil jammed his gun trying to re-load his bullets of mass destruction. Now God can shoot back with his bullets. These bullets bring hope to situations that appear unsalvageable. Once my husband and I put down the devil's tools, we were able to start loving one another God's way. We used **1 Corinthians 13** as our foundation to rebuild. Take a moment to read this passage of scripture before diving into the Call to Action Activities Section and the second part of the showdown between the devil and God as they battle it out over our marriage.

The Greatest Gift

Though I speak with the tongues of men and of angels but have not **love**, I have become sounding brass or a clanging cymbal. And though I have *the gift of* prophecy, and understand all mysteries and all knowledge, and though I have all faith, so that I could remove mountains, but have not **love**, I am nothing. And though I bestow all my goods to feed *the poor,* and though I give my body to be burned, but have not **love**, it profits me nothing. **Love** suffers long *and* is kind; **love** does not envy; **love** does not parade itself, is not puffed up; does not behave rudely, does not seek its own, is not provoked, thinks no evil; does not rejoice in iniquity, but rejoices in the truth; bears all things, believes all things, hopes all things, endures all things. **Love** never fails. But whether *there are* prophecies, they will fail; whether *there are* tongues, they will cease; whether *there is* knowledge, it will vanish away. For we know in part and we prophesy in part. But when that which is perfect has come, then that which is in part will be done away. When I was a child, I spoke as a child, I understood as a child, I thought as a child; but when I became a man, I put away childish things. For now, we see in a mirror, dimly, but then face to face. Now I know in part, but then I shall know just as I also am known. And now abide faith, hope, **love**, these three; but the greatest of these *is* **LOVE**.

Call to Action

This section of the intermission is designed for the creation of dialogue between you and your spouse. The key to spiritual freedom is accepting what is. The more you talk about what hinders you, the freedom you will experience. It's important, to be honest, and open with one another so that the healing process can begin.

Exercise – Letting Go of the Past

1. What are some things in your past that you have not let go of?

2. Was there some emotional trauma that you are still holding on to?

3. Do you find yourself sitting in the seat of blame?

4. Are there things you have not forgiven your partner for?

Activity – Putting the Blame to Shame (3-part activity)

Part 1 The Shoot-Out

Directions: For this activity, you will need two chairs and an honest heart. Choose who will go first. Once you have completed the activity, it's your partner's turn. When you both have had a turn, let the dialogue flow.

Face your partner and tell them the things you have blamed them for.

"I have blamed you for: _____"

"Can you forgive me for blaming you for these things?"

"Today I choose to let go of the blame. From this day forward, I am choosing to forgive you."

"What are some things you have blamed me for?"

Part 2 Burn the Evidence

Directions: This challenge can be done indoors or outdoors (whichever is comfortable for you). Write down on a piece of paper the things you blamed your partner for. Make sure to add "unforgiveness" to your list. Use your fireplace or sink to "burn the evidence".

Part 3 Close the Case on "The Past" with Prayer

Use the space below to write out a personal prayer to help deal with your past.

_____

_____

_____

_____

_____

_____

_____

_____

_____

_____

_____

_____

_____

_____

_____

_____

Exercise – Dealing with Rejection

Think back on a situation where you felt rejected and write it in the space provided below or use a separate piece of paper.

1. What emotions did you experience?

2. How did these emotions affect your judgment?

3. What are your conditions of satisfaction for being accepted?

4. Do you feel you have to be perfect?

5. Are you masking your weaknesses so others can't see them?

6. How can you use rejection as a learning opportunity?

Activity – Removing the Mask of Rejection (3-Part activity)

Part 1 The Shoot-Out

Directions: For this activity, you will need two chairs, a masquerade mask if you have one or a scarf, and an honest heart. Place your chairs back-to-back. "Masking" creates walls. When you sit in the chairs, your backs facing each other will serve as the wall. Put your masks on. Choose who will go first. Once you have completed the activity, it's your partner's turn. When you both have had a turn, let the dialogue flow.

Repeat this pattern as many times as you need to until both of you have taken a turn. The objective of this activity is to gain an understanding of how your partner experiences rejection from you. In the exchange, you learn what your partner needs to help them overcome rejection in your marriage.

You: "I feel rejected when you_____."

Your Partner: "What do you need from me to change this feeling?"

You: "I need_____."

Your Partner: "I understand what you need. Please give me the opportunity to give you what you need."

After the activity is complete, face one another, remove your masks, and talk about what you got out of the activity.

Part 2 Throw Away the Evidence of Rejection

This challenge can be done indoors. Write out the negative feelings/emotions you dealt with from your partner's rejection. Exchange lists and discuss the feelings/emotions that are listed on your partner's paper. Throw away the list.

Part 3 Close the Case on "Masking the Rejection" with Prayer

Use the space below to write out a personal prayer to help you deal with rejection.

_____

_____

_____

_____

_____

_____

_____

_____

Exercise – Trust Issues

1. Do you trust yourself?

2. In what ways have you not trusted your spouse?

3. What hinders you from completely trusting your spouse and God?

4. Do you feel that not trusting your spouse is a direct reflection of you not trusting God?

5. Do you allow doubt to get in the way of you trusting God?

6. How have you let your traumatic experiences distort your views of your spouse?

7. In what ways do you cause division between you and your spouse?

Activity – Building Trust

Part 1 The Shoot-Out

Directions: For this activity, you will need your kitchen table, eye contact, and an honest heart. Sit across from one another and grab hands. This activity requires direct eye contact. Choose who will go first. Once you have completed the activity, it's your partner's turn. When you both have had a turn, let the dialogue flow.

You only get to ask 3 questions.

"I always wanted to know but I was too afraid to ask_____?"

Give your partner the chance to respond to each question. After you hear their response, take a moment to process what you heard. Create your reassurance statement when all questions have been answered:

"Thank you for sharing. I reassure you that I will not internalize what you shared, and I will not retaliate."

Part 2 Get Rid of the Evidence

Work with your partner to come up with a way to get rid of your trust issues. Be creative!

Part 3 Close the Case on "Trust Issues" with Prayer

Use the space below to write out a personal prayer to help you deal with your trust issues.

_____

_____

_____

_____

_____

_____

_____

_____

_____

_____

_____

_____

_____

_____

_____

...End Of Intermission

Bullet 4

Rebuilding God's Way

Using the word of God on The Road to Recovery

God entered the shoot out and fought on behalf of my husband and me. Both of us were living in different places. I think we were in denial regarding our six-month separation. My husband was staying with his brother and I was at my aunt's house. We would communicate from time-to-time through texting. Our phone conversation was very limited by choice. The less we talked, the less likely chance we had to argue. Once God stepped in, He started to deal with our hearts at the same time regarding our broken marriage. This was a clear sign that although we were apart, we were still connected to one another in the spiritual realm.

I missed my husband but anger and hurt hindered me from wanting to be in his presence. And I'm sure the feeling was mutual for him. He would text me sometimes to tell me he missed me. The first few months of uncoupling, I remember crying and being angry with God about my marital situation. The lack of understanding made me question God and why He allowed this to happen. I didn't know the ins and outs of what my husband was doing or how he really felt about this ordeal because we weren't together. Five months into me blaming everyone but myself for the dissipation of my marriage, God shut my mouth from the negative communication and told me to pray. So, I spent the last month of our separation praying for my marriage.

Now, this is what God spoke to me as I prayed every day for Him to heal our broken hearts and reunite us as one. He told me that I needed to repent for not trusting him and for taking matters into my own hands. Next, He said he is bringing us both to a point of decision. I really didn't understand what God meant by this, but I continued praying. He left the decision of us being together in our hands.

Moment of Revelation – It was never in God's will for us to separate, but he trusted us to make the right decision for our marriage. How is it that God can trust us for something as important as this, but we can't trust Him with our life?

God continued to speak as I prayed. He said he was going to bring us back together and that things would be different this time around. He was requiring both of us to change for the better. He gave me specific instructions on finding a couple's therapist that He would use to help us through the issues we were having in our marriage. He said the first thing we must work on is the rebuilding of our marriage. So, let's dive into the first bullet God shot back at the devil – REBUILDING.

There is a process to rebuilding but first, let's find out what it means. Merriam-Webster defines "rebuilding" as the process of making extensive repairs to, reconstructing. It also means to rebuild something again after it has been damaged or destroyed. While reading the definition, a scripture came to mind – *Matthew 21:42 Jesus said to them, "Have you never read in the*

Scriptures: The stone which the builders rejected has now become the chief cornerstone. This was the LORD's doing, and it is marvelous in our eyes? Because God is who He is, He understands that, for something to be rebuilt, it must be torn down. To give you a full understanding of what God had to do to rebuild our marriage in the spiritual realm, I want to breakdown what a carpenter does in the natural realm.

Carpenters build and some of their core skills include math skills, physical strength, communication, attention to detail, problem-solving, dexterity, and mechanical skills. Their list of tools consists of a power drill, saw, sander, hammer, nails, tape measure, and a stud finder. The most important core skill of a carpenter is their ability to read blueprints. Blueprints contain important details of the construction project. They enable the engineers and carpenters to design with the "bigger picture" in mind. A carpenter must use precision when building. If a measurement is slightly off or if a nail is not hammered in the correct place during framing, the entire building is going to be off. When this happens, the carpenter must tear the building down and rebuild it. God's rebuilding process is like that of a carpenter. He has the blueprint for our life, he saw the bigger picture before he formed us. *Jeremiah 1:5 - Before I formed you in the womb, I knew you; before you were born, I sanctified you; I ordained you a prophet to the nations.* The Master Carpenter has tools such as a saw, plane, and chisel. He uses His tools with precision and depth. The difference between God and a regular carpenter is that God builds with perfection! Pay close attention as you see how God reconstructed our marriage with the saw, plane, and chisel.

The "Saw" Shell Casing

Life tore my marriage to pieces! We developed holes and cracks in our foundation. Our marriage's covering had blown with the winds from the many trials and tribulations we'd gone through. We were exposed since we didn't have a covering, and because of this, there were some ungodly seeds that took root in the soul of our marriage and began to grow. Our foundation was in serious need of repair and a spiritual circumcision had to be done in the soul of our union. A saw is a tool God uses to cut measured pieces of His strength and love that our foundation needed. It was also used to cut and prune away the damaged areas in the foundation that had not yielded any fruit – the ungodly seeds related to the pains of our past (contention, pride, anger, bitterness, unfor-giveness, and strife). Pruning is a technique used to cut away dead branches and stems, es-pecially to increase fruitfulness and growth. God had to tear down our way of thinking and our way of doing things. He stripped us from the inside out. Although quite painful, it had to be done. Anything that's been cut and pruned must be smoothed over. And God has just the right tool for this.

The "Plane" Shell Casing

A plane is a tool that is used to smooth rough edges. It provides a distinguished look to the previously cut pieces that were cut by the saw. The plane is also used for shaping and forming, resulting in a smooth surface. The same way a carpenter uses sandpaper to smooth a piece of wood after it has been cut is the same way God used His spiritual plane to smooth the areas of our foundation where the damage had been cut away and pruned. Once the cutting and pruning were complete, He me-ticulously laid the polished pieces in place, making sure to fill every crack and hole with His Word, strength, and love. The more and more God filled the holes and cracks, the more strength I gained. During the separation, I remember times I prayed. I felt the strength of God all over me. His unadulterated love slowly penetrated my heart. My tears of sorrow became tears of joy. My warfare was now directed at the devil and not my husband. But this was only the beginning of the rebuilding process. Let's see what the last tool was that God used to complete the foundation.

The "Chisel" Shell Casing

I mentioned earlier that ungodly seeds had taken root into the soul of our marriage that needed to be uprooted. The perfect tool for this was God's chisel. His chisel was a special kind of material that could pierce and cut through a hard surface. For the repairing of our foundation, it was used to dig around the stony ground of the ungodly seeds so that they could be plucked up. I don't know about you, but it's a very difficult thing when God puts a mirror in front of you so that you can see yourself. There is nowhere to run or hide. Your ugly parts have been exposed for you to deal with accordingly. He was exposing for the greater good of our marriage. It was up to us to make the necessary changes for the healing process to keep flowing. God used seeds of righteousness from his word to plant in the holes where the ungodly seeds had been plucked up. Once these seeds took root, the fruit of His spirit (*Galatians 5:22-23 Love, joy, peace, longsuffering, kindness, goodness, faithfulness, longsuffering, and self-control*) began to grow in our foundation.

Take Away

It was important for God to completely repair the foundation before the covering was put in place. He made sure the devil could not shoot any more bullets into our union. I bet you are wondering what God used for the covering…. you guessed it! He used Himself. When my husband and I stopped arguing, fault finding and complaining, God was able to come back into our hearts. We began to read our Bible more and more each day. Prayer became a movement in our life. I'd lost hope when we first separated, but as God began the repairs, hope slowly made its way back into our marriage. There were other things God used to put the finishing touches on our foundation. Fire was used to treat the foundation and burn the impurities which was the leftover residue from our past. The file He used served as His mercy. It broke up the fallow ground of our hearts and softened the edges. Lastly, oil (God's anointing) was applied as a protection to beautify the foundation. God's Masterpiece was complete and I began to see the light at the end of the tunnel! We were finally on the road to recovery.

Bullet 5

Communication is Key

Relearning the Art of Communication

The key to understanding communication is knowing what it means. Webster-Merriam's Dictionary defines communication as a process by which information is exchanged between individuals through a common system of symbols, signs, or behavior. The different types of communication include listening, verbal communication, non-verbal communication, emotional awareness, written communication, and lastly, communicating in difficult situations. Communication may be different for you and your spouse due to different backgrounds, cultures, and experiences. The key to getting through the rough patches is strong communication, and it's a part of your foundation. Any good and healthy marriage thrives on an even, open exchange of beliefs, desires, and positive emotions.

There were many different situations that showed my husband and me that we were bad communicators. Our main vice when disagreements would arise was shutting down. My biggest hindrance was my mouth. Yep, my mouth! When my husband said something I didn't like, there was no backing down from me. I didn't know how to walk away and not say anything or let it go. Something in me always had to respond. He would always tell me it was the way I said things that made him shut down and because I was not on the receiving end of the conversation, I couldn't understand what he meant. It did not register to me that the way I say things were harsh and insensitive.

My words hitting his ears seemed as if I didn't care about his feelings. The only thing running through my mind during the heat of an argument with my husband is how I allowed my ex-husband to take away my voice. I refused to allow that to happen in this marriage. So every time we had a disagreement, I found myself speaking my mind to no end. My husband's way of shutting me down happened every time he dismissed my feelings about something we were disputing about. This infuriated me and he knew it! I'm not sure if what I was saying hit a nerve with him or if he just didn't want to hear what I was saying. Either way, it seemed as if my feelings didn't matter to him. We both listened to react, not respond. And then one day it hit me and God spoke to me.

Moment of Revelation – You cannot be submissive to God and not be submissive to your spouse. All sin is disobedience, even not submitting. Especially, when God said it in His word in *Ephesians 5:22 - For wives, this means submit to your husbands as to the Lord.*

Ladies, I'm sorry to say that even when it comes to communicating with your spouse, you must submit. You may not always agree with what they say, but you must follow the word of God. God goes on to say that submission should be a mutual thing between husbands and wives. A husband is to love his spouse just as Christ loved the church and just as much as he loves his own body. This is how he submits. If a man loves his body, he loves himself. He will definitely know how to treat his wife and love her, especially in the art of communicating with her. His communication will be with love and tenderness.

Ephesians 4:29 says don't use foul or abusive language. Let everything you say be good and helpful so that your words will be an encouragement to those who hear them. My husband didn't really have an issue with how he said things but I did. So I can only talk about this from my perspective and how God had to tame my mouth. He made me realize that my tone wasn't always pleasant. My harshness and displeasing tone came from a place of brokenness. Where did the brokenness take place? You guessed it right again, my past. I felt the need to be overly assertive because I didn't have a voice in past relationships. And it's the same thing for my husband. His dismissal of my feelings came from his past and how he didn't trust women.

1 Timothy 2:11 tells us as wives to learn quietly and submissively. If taken out of context, this scripture can start a war in a marriage. But all God is saying is that we must settle disagreements with peacefulness, stillness, and calmness.

The "Peace" Shell Casing

One key principle to help settle things within a marriage peacefully is knowing your spouse. You must develop knowledge of your spouse's personality. You can learn a lot through observation but to really get down to the nitty-gritty of who your significant other is, you must go to God in prayer to find out their heart. Knowing what bothers them and what excites them is very important. What might not bother you may be annoying to them. What may excite you, may not be as exhilarating to them. Not knowing can cause a disruption in their peace. If you are constantly doing things they don't like, their peace is shaken almost to the point where it can become tormenting. We must do what Jesus would do and that is to *work at living in peace with everyone, and work at living a holy life, for those who are not holy will not see the Lord – Hebrews 12:14.* There is nothing like a marriage filled with peacefulness and blissfulness!

The Still" Shell Casing

Experiencing true intimacy with God as a couple requires you to quiet the noise in your union and enter His stillness together. How will you understand what it means to accept and honor or understand your mate as the man or the woman God made them to be? This principle is important because it is a common source that leads to miscommunication, the simple fact of realizing that men and women are insanely different. When there is no understanding and acceptance of differences, arguments ensue, and all communication goes out the window!

Psalm 46:10 declares for us to *be still and know that I am God.* Stillness in this scripture means that you must let go of the frustration, hostility, and fear that was birthed during the angry communication. You must let go of the feelings of resentment at the apparent injustice caused by something your spouse said that hurt you. Instead of dishonoring one another with your words, you must learn to see your mate as God sees them. Again, the only way to achieve this is through true intimacy with God on an individual level, so that when you come together to pray, you are bringing acceptance and understanding of what is needed for your union to be able to effectively communicate.

The "Calm" Shell Casing

Using edifying words is the last principle that will be discussed when it comes to communication. Edifying is essential because it has the ability to bring calmness to any disruptive communication where disrespect and dishonor have taken place. Uplifting words reduce stress and bring peace. Even in those times where you want to let all evilness come out of your mouth during an argument, you must refrain. Sometimes you just have to take time to quiet your mind so that you can bridle your tongue. Having an unbridled tongue means that you are under no tolerable restraint and it is absolute evidence that you are hypocritical and vain in speech. Find the peace within to soothe your thoughts; doing this will teach you how to communicate with calmness.

Take Away

Why not learn from God, the author of the Bible who spoke His living word into existence! Just like God, we have the power to speak into existence a beautiful harmonious prosperous marriage that glorifies God. Or, we can use our communicated words to destroy the very gift and mission that God has given you in marriage. Remember the saying "sticks and stones may break my bones but words will never hurt me?" Satan is the father of all lies and this is one lie that causes many to carry hurt and pain for years to come. You can communicate so negatively that you affect your spouse's destiny. *Proverbs 18:21 states the tongue can bring death or life; those who love to talk will reap the consequences.* So be careful how you say things and watch your tone. If you would be offended by it, then you should not communicate it to your spouse. Lastly, *let your conversation* (communication) *be gracious and attractive so that you will have the right response for everyone – Colossians 4:6.*

Bullet 6

Two is Better Than One

Joining Forces to Fight the Problem, Not One Another

Have you ever heard the saying that two is better than one? There is no definition needed here because, although a cliché', it's true. This five-worded phrase explains itself and says that God's grace is enough in any and everything that you and your spouse may go through. The number five means "grace" in the spiritual realm. *2 Corinthians 12:9 – each time he said, "My grace is all you need. My power works best in weakness." So now I am glad to boast about my weaknesses so that the power of Christ can work through me.* This is God's assurance to you and your spouse that He is all that you need no matter what! No problem is too big for God. When issues surface, you and your spouse must work together with God to find a resolution. Think about it…. after you have argued and blamed one another, what did you really accomplish? Did you reach a resolution to whatever you are/were facing? Did either of you accept responsibility for your part in the problem? These are questions you must ask yourself. Operating as one consists of you being on one accord with your spouse to accomplish the same goal. Remember, being married with an individual mindset is not of God.

Amos 3:3 says, can two people walk together without agreeing on the direction? What do you think God is saying here? What he is saying is that despite your differences, there must be a willingness to walk your marriage out. Willingness is defined by the Oxford Languages dictionary as the quality or state of being prepared to do something, readiness. The only way two people traveling in the same exact direction at the same exact time will meet is through divine intervention. It's no accident that my husband and I got married. God had us both on a journey down the same road at the same time. Even though there were obstacles along the way, God's appointed time allowed us to cross each other's path. Our spirit was in agreement with God as He ordered our steps. Once we met and decided to get together, we came into an agreement based on many factors but mainly because of our beliefs and love for one another.

As a single person I used to say that in order for a man to get to my heart, he had to go through God first. I prayed for a God-fearing man who loved God. In him loving God, I knew he would love me and my children. He also prayed for a God-fearing woman who would love him unconditionally, through all his flaws and failures. He wanted a godly woman who knew how to pray for him and who knew how to pray him through difficult situations he was facing. We didn't know at that time that this meeting was ordained by God. It just felt right to us.

Moment of Revelation – To the natural eye, our paths were different. But because God ordained our union, no matter what direction we went in and how many times we got off course, it was Him who led us to each other.

The "Agreement" Shell Casing

Earlier in this chapter I talked about the scripture found in Amos 3:3, how can two walk together except they agree? Now contrary to the question, can two people walk together without agreeing on the direction, is this: two people cannot walk together if they don't agree. Conflict will always be present because of their differences. No, you will not agree with your spouse on everything, but the basis of this scripture is saying that you must agree on the principle thing in order to walk together in the same direction. According to the Oxford Languages Dictionary, an agreement can be defined as harmony or accordance in opinion or feeling; a position or result of agreeing; a negotiated and typically legally binding arrangement between parties as to a course of action; the absence of incompatibility between two things;

consistency. Two parallel lines will never intersect. Although they share many points along the way. They can travel alongside one another infinitely and never intersect. When there is a disagreement between you and your spouse, you hinder the process of getting to the resolution of things. The only way you and your spouse will intersect or come into an agreement when there are differences is to bring God into the equation. As you agree in prayer, God will provide direction on how to resolve the problem.

The "Prayer Shell" Casing

Prayer is the ultimate assault against the devil! *Matthew 18:20 says that where two or three gather together as my followers, I am there among them.* Look at what we have here – another point proving that two are better than one. Often times, couples fight against one another, leaving themselves open for the devil to come in and sift them as wheat. One major lesson my husband and I had to learn was that our fight wasn't against each other it was against the devil. We had to hide *Ephesians 6:12* in our hearts – *For we are not fighting against flesh-and-blood enemies, but against evil rulers and authorities of the unseen world, against mighty powers in this dark world, and against evil spirits in the heavenly places. Ephesians 6:13-18, God's whole armor (helmet of salvation, breastplate of righteousness, the belt of truth, the sword of the spirit, and the shoes of peace).* This scripture is needed for spiritual warfare as you unite with your mate in prayer. Just like praise confuses the enemy, so does prayer. When you and your spouse pray together, the dunamis power of God is released. You are not praying in your strength or ability; God's power is being unleashed through you to produce a supernatural manifestation of miracles, signs, and wonders for your marriage. As your prayer life develops and stays consistent, the peace of God will enter your marriage. *Philippians 4:6-7 says don't worry about anything; instead, pray about everything. Tell God what you need, and thank him for all he has done. Then you will experience God's peace, which exceeds anything we can understand. His peace will guard your hearts and minds as you live in Christ Jesus.*

The Conditions of Intimacy and Union in Your Marriage with God

1. In order for you and your spouse to walk together in love and fulfill the sacred covenant that you made with God through marriage, there must be harmony regarding the scriptures and what they say about marriage. The husband and wife must acquiesce in what God has solemnly declared and imposed.

2. There must be a correlation of viewpoints regarding the rule by which redeemed believers are to be governed; your spiritual duties must be fulfilled towards God.

3. Husband and wife cannot walk together unless there is a mutual reverence for God. You and your spouse are to acknowledge His lordship in every area of your life and obey what He commands.

Take Away

Why are two better than one? *Ecclesiastes 4:9-12 says two people are better off than one, for they can help each other succeed. If one person falls, the other can reach out and help. But someone who falls alone is in real trouble. Likewise, two people lying close together can keep each other warm. But how can one be warm alone? A person standing alone can be attacked and defeated, but two can stand back-to-back and conquer. Three are even better, for a triple-braided cord is not easily broken.* This scripture seals your destiny when God is in the midst of your union. His supernatural power takes control of any development of events that are beyond your control. He defeats the powers of the devil over your marriage and restores the hope, love, and peace that was stolen during the battle. Finally, above all, it's God's will that you love one another, for it is LOVE that conquers all!

About the Author

Sharee currently resides in Atlanta, Georgia. Born in St. Louis, MO, she gained a love for writing through the many different books she read from her adolescent days to her teen years. Poetry was her first interest as a writer. As time continued and as Sharee began to experience life, the thoughts of writing a book became more and more real to her. She sat down and began writing, not a poem this time, but something much deeper and personal. She didn't stop writing until her first book was birthed, titled "This So-Called Single Life". This book journeyed through her life after divorce, detailing real and true events, such as her abusive first marriage. It dealt with being single after a very grueling divorce, all while working, dating, and raising 3 children on my own. Sharee shares her dating pitfalls and life lessons that were learned along the way. She also wrote a journal to accompany this book, titled "This So-Called Single Life Journal Experience". Sharee wants her readers to experience her life as they journal their personal experiences while reading her book.

It is from the different events in her 2nd marriage that Sharee was able to write her third book titled "Before the Shot". This book speaks about breaking the cycle of broken relationships, healing from your past, and walking into the marriage that God ordained you to have. Sharee is now happily married to a wonderful man by the name of Jerron Smith. They have a total of five grown children, whom they love dearly, ranging in age from 18-24. In her spare time, she loves to write, listen to music, and spend time with family. Although she works in IT at a well-known university, nothing trumps her love for writing! She hopes that her books touch your life in a fulfilling way.

www.ingramcontent.com/pod-product-compliance
Lightning Source LLC
Chambersburg PA
CBHW051432090426
42737CB00014B/2933